World's Greatest SCIENTISTS & INVENTORS of All History

This book belongs to:

_____

Scientific discoveries over the centuries have helped shape the way we live today. Without pioneering scientists working towards cures for diseases, new inventions, and better ways to do things, life today would be different. Here are some of the most influential visionaries throughout history, organized in chronological order, who have made a significant contribution to the scientific community and to our everyday lives.

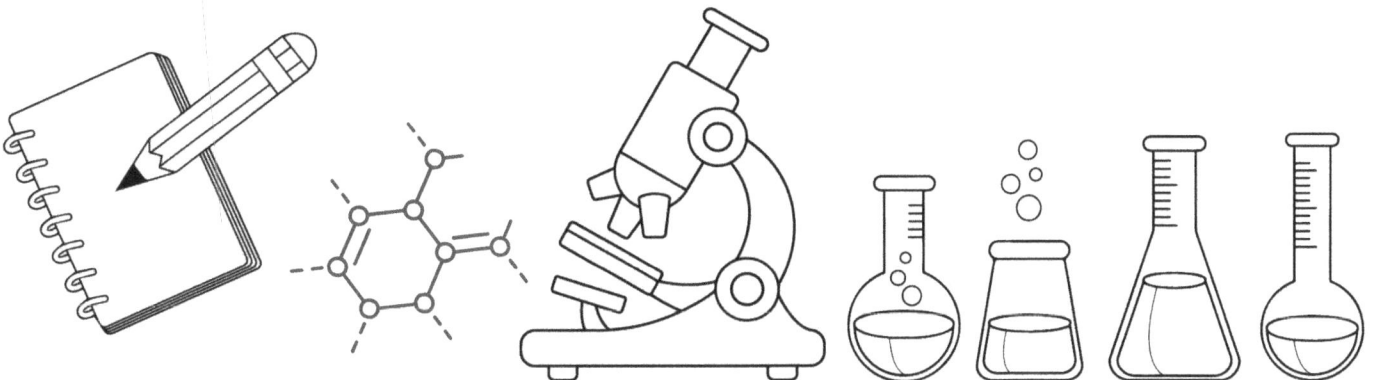

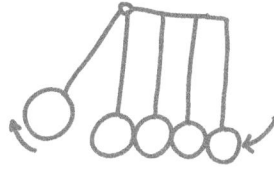

Scientists of Antiquity

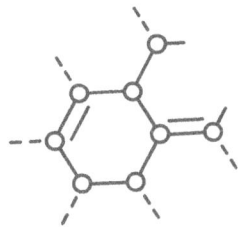

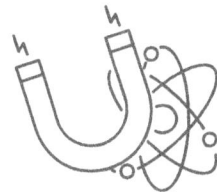

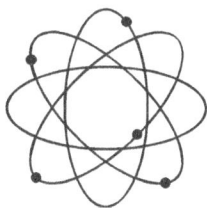

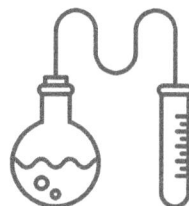

Hippocrates
(c.460 BC – c.370 BC)

Nationality: Greek

Known for: Father of Medicine

Credited with writing the Hippocratic Oath that today's medical professionals still follow in their practice.

He had the theory of the vapors, which stated that many diseases were the result of a bad diet.

Aristotle

(384 BC – 322 BC)

Nationality: Greek
Known for: Theory of Three Psyches, Scientific Method
Wrote about many scientific topics, including biology,
physics, and zoology. His ideas helped shape
Western scientific thought into the Renaissance
until they were replaced with Newtonian physics.

Archimedes

(c.287 BC – c.212 BC)

Nationality: Greek
Known for: Archimedes Principle, Archimedes Screw
Astronomer, scientist, and physicist with several inventions to his name. He created a formula to calculate the area of the underside of a parabola. In addition, he designed many machines of antiquity.

Galen
(c. 129 AD – 200/216 AD)

Nationality: Roman
Known for: Father of Medicine
Galen was best known as Galen of Pergamon. He was a famous philosopher and surgeon amongst the Romans. His works contributed greatly to the knowledge of anatomy, pathology, physiology, neurology, pharmacology, logic, and philosophy.

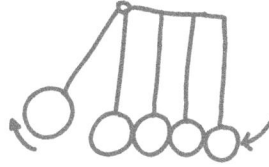

Scientists of the Middle Ages

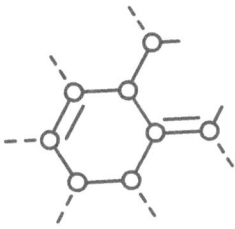

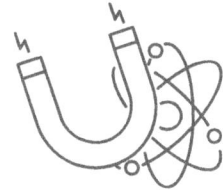

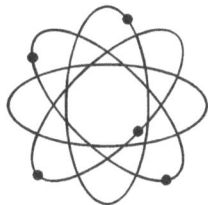

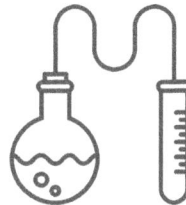

Leonardo da Vinci

(1452-1519)

Nationality: Italian
Known for: Vitruvian man, aerial screw
Renaissance thinker who made several inventions and discoveries
in the fields of engineering, anatomy, and hydrodynamics. Also,
one of the most well-known artists throughout history.

Nicolaus Copernicus

(1473-1543)

Nationality: Polish
Known for: Heliocentric Model of the Universe
Astronomer and mathematician from the Renaissance era. He
theorized that the sun was the center of the universe rather
than the Earth, which was a controversial claim at the time.

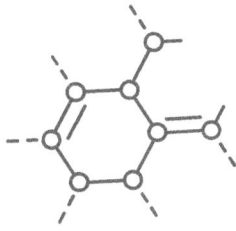
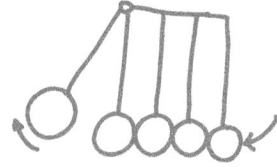

Scientists of the Scientific Revolution

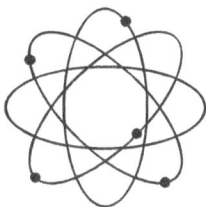
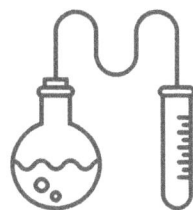
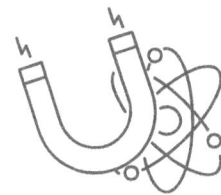

Galileo Galilei

(1564-1642)

Nationality: Italian
Known for: Father of Modern Science; Heliocentrism
Astronomer, physicist, mathematician, and philosopher who said the earth and planets revolve around the sun. He confirmed the different phases of Venus with a telescope and observed sunspots and the moons of Jupiter.

Johannes Kepler

(1571-1630)

Nationality: German

Known for: Laws of Planetary Motion

Defined a new type of astronomy called "celestial physics," which said that God created the world in a way that can only be studied through reasoning. Also developed the Keplerian Telescope, which was an improvement on previous telescopes.

Evangelista Torricelli

(1608-1647)

Nationality: Italian
Known for: Invented the barometer Mathematician and physicist
who built several telescopes and microscopes. He is also known for
creating the barometer and Torricelli's Law. He also studied and
produced scientific evidence for the causes of wind.

Blaise Pascal

(1623-1662)

Nationality: French
Known for: Modern theories of probabilities Mathematician and phycisist who is credited with making the first usable calculator, called the Pascaline. He published a treatise on projective geometry and is known for his work in mathematical probability theories.

Robert Boyle

(1627-1691)

Nationality: English
Known for: Boyle's Law Physicist and chemist who is partially credited with creating the field of modern chemistry. Boyle's Law refers to the relationship between a gas and pressure in a closed system when the temperature remains the same.

Isaac Newton

(1642-1727)

Nationality: British
Known for: Laws of Gravity and Motion
Newton is one of the most influential scientists in history. He published several books, formulated several scientific laws, and made significant discoveries. His main credits include formulating the laws of gravitation and motion.

Edmond Halley

(1656-1742)

Nationality: English
Known for: Calculated the orbit of Halley's Comet
Mathematician and astronomer who published important papers on
topics like sunspots, the solar system and more. He is also known
for trying to measure the distance from the earth to the sun
based on the travels of Venus.

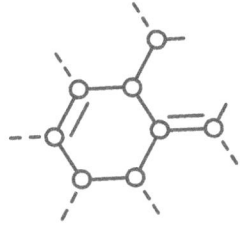

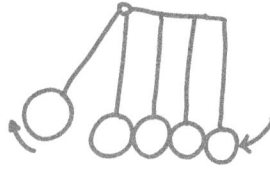

Scientists of the Age of Enlightenment

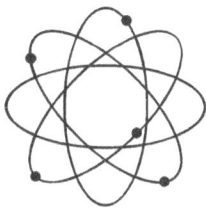

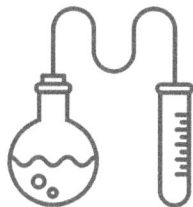

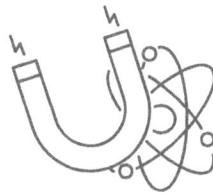

Anders Celsius

(1701-1744)

Nationality: Swedish
Known for: Proposed the Celsius scale for temperatures
Astronomer and professor who studied temperature and the
connection between the aurora borealis and the planet's magnetic
field. Published findings that noted that part of Scandinavia was
rising above sea level.

James Watt

(1736-1819)

Nationality: Scottish
Known for: Electrical unit Watt named after him
Mechanical engineer and inventor who improved the efficiency of
the steam engine through the use of a separate condenser.
Watt also developed the idea of horsepower.

Edward Jenner

(1749-1823)

Nationality: English
Known for: Pioneered the smallpox vaccine Often called the
"Father of Immunology," his research in vaccinations have saved
countless lives over the last couple centuries. He was appointed
to be official physician to King George IV in 1821.

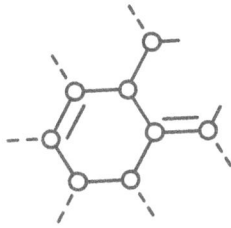

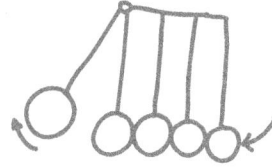

Scientists of the 19th Century

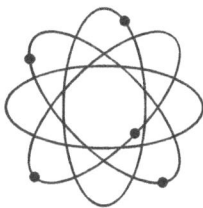

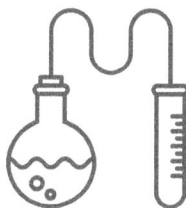

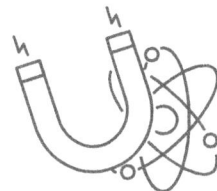

Michael Faraday

(1791-1867)

Nationality: British
Known for: Discovered electromagnetic induction
Physicist and chemist who worked to make electricity a viable
technology that could be used. He also did a lot of work with
batteries, electrolysis, and magnets.

Charles Babbage

(1791-1871)

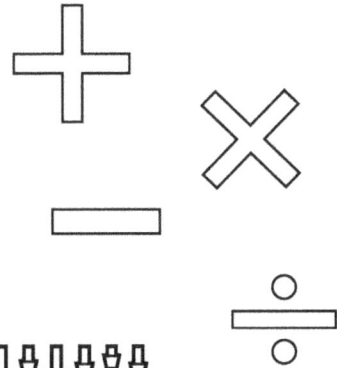

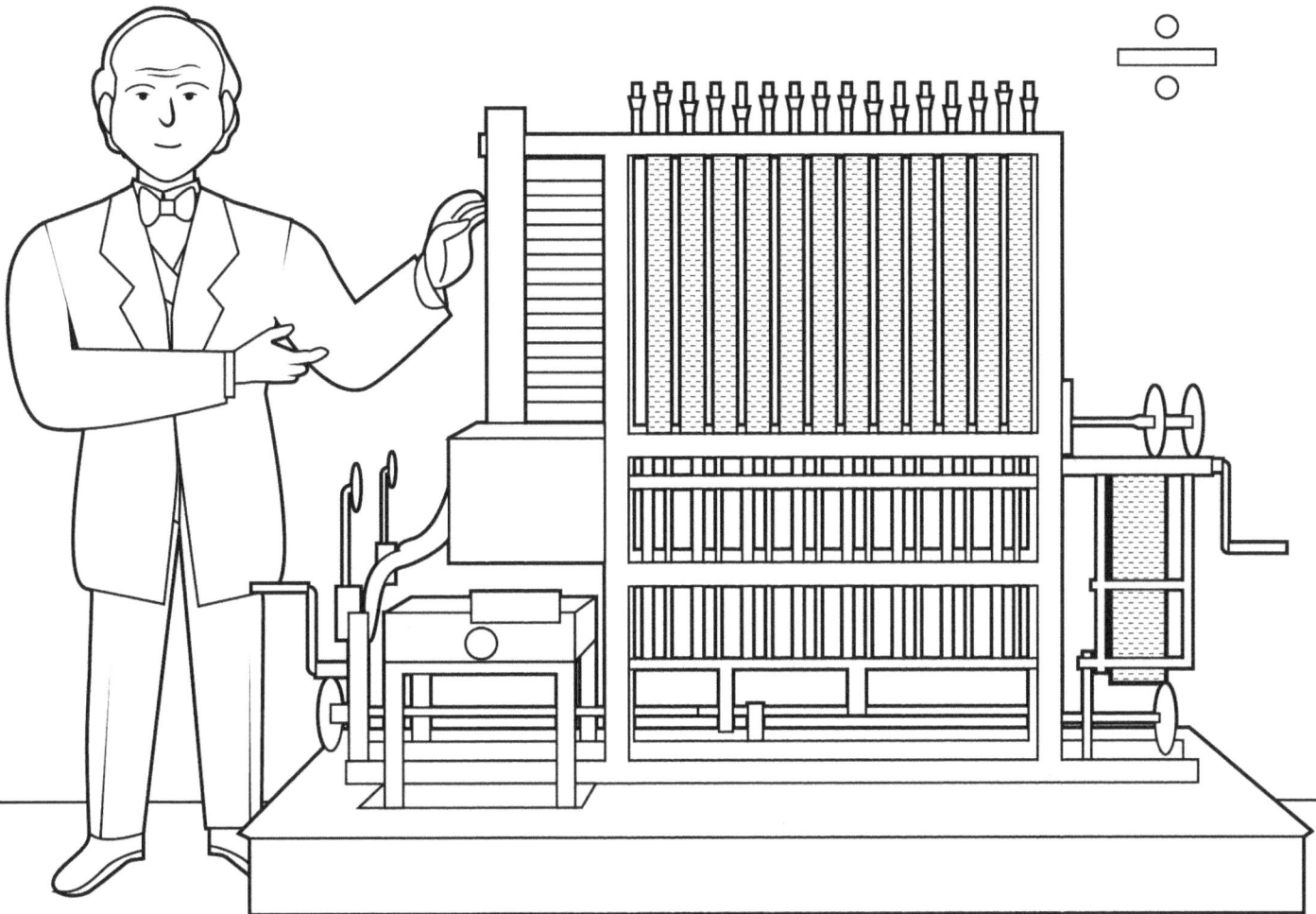

Nationality: British
Known for: Charles Babbage was a British mathematician and computer scientist. He designed and developed a mechanical calculator capable of calculating tables of numerical functions by the method of differences.

Thomas Graham

(1805-1869)

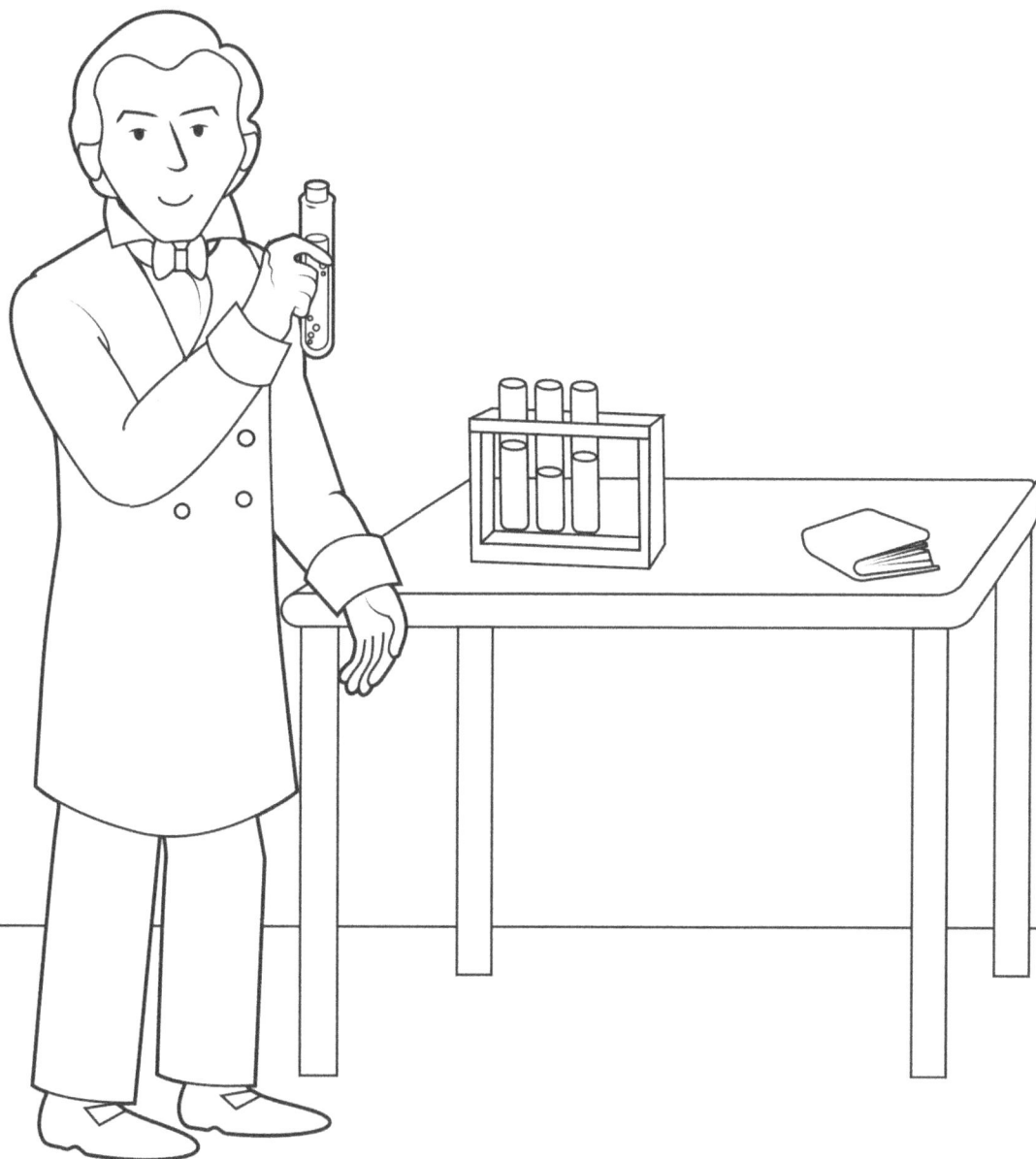

Nationality: Scottish
Known for: Invented the dialysis process for kidneys
Chemist who studied the diffusion of gasses. He coined Graham's
Law and, also, developed the process of dialysis, which is still used
in medical facilities today. Graham is also credited with being the
founder of colloid chemistry.

Charles Darwin

(1809-1882)

Nationality: British
Known for: Theory of Evolution and Natural Selection
Darwin formulated a theory that said humans descended from animals through a process called Natural Selection. His ideas have created a great deal of controversy in his day and through today.

Louis Pasteur

(1822-1895)

Nationality: French
Known for: Process of Pasteurization, vaccine for anthrax and rabies Influential in the field of medical microbiology. Pasteur worked toward cures for diseases and processing methods for reducing harmful bacteria in milk, wine, and other products.His work also helped reduce mortality rates from puerperal fever.

Gregor Mendel

(1822-1884)

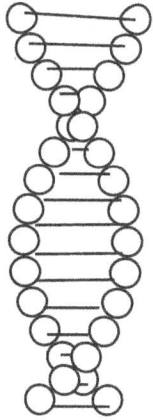

Nationality: Austrian
Known for: Father of Modern Genetics Scientist who experimented with plant hybridizations. He discovered that many of his findings could be transferred to animals and humans. Coined the terms "recessive" and "dominant" when referring to genes.

William Thomson Kelvin

(1824-1907)

Nationality: British
Known for: Kelvin Scale of Temperature Physicist and engineer who determined the value for absolute zero in regards to temperature. He also estimated that the age of the earth was between 20 and 400 million years old and helped develop the second law of thermodynamics.

Alfred Nobel

(1824-1896)

Nationality: Swedish
Known for: Invented dynamite Best known for the Nobel Prizes, which are named after him and generally awarded to those who excel in the sciences. These prizes are often reserved for those who make a significant discovery or invention in their respective fields.

Ernst Haeckel

(1834-1919)

Nationality: German
Known for: Gave names to thousands of unknown species Zoologist who supported Darwin's theories regarding evolution and developed the recapitulation theory, also known as the biogenetic law. He also created several terms in the field of biology, including stem cell, ecology, and several others.

Dmitri Mendeleev

(1834-1907)

Nationality: Russian
Known for: Periodic Table Published Principles of Chemistry in 1869 which detailed his work in arranging the various elements according to their atomic mass. He is also credited with introducing the metric system to the Russian Empire.

Wilhelm Conrad Rontgen

(1845-1923)

Nationality: German
Known for: Discovered the modern-day x-rays
Physicist who worked with electromagnetic radiation. He won the
Nobel Prize in Physics in 1901 for his discovery of x-rays. he also
worked extensively with magnetic fields, although his findings in
this field are lesser known.

Thomas Edison

(1847-1931)

Nationality: American
Known for: Phonograph; electric light bulb; motion pictures; etc.
Edison created some of the most prominent inventions that are
in most households today. He often gets credit for being the
person who created the first research laboratory and he held
more than 1,000 patents for his inventions.

Nikola Tesla

(1856-1943)

Nationality: Croatian
Known for: A/C Electrical System.
Created precursors to modern-day inventions, including a global communication system and induction motors, among others.
Tesla experimented with radio communications and x-rays, too. He was considered a "mad scientist" because of his unique inventions.

Max Planck

(1858-1947)

Nationality: German
Known for: Quantum Theory
Theoretical physicist who won the Nobel Prize in Physics in 1918 for his theory on quantum physics. He revolutionized the way people thought about the atomic process.

George Washington Carver

(1864-1943)

Nationality: American
Known for: Used peanuts in a variety of inventions and products
Scientist and botanist who strived to create alternative crops
for sweet potatoes, peanuts, cotton and soybeans. He also helped
establish a foundation in his name at the Tuskegee Institute and he
became a member of England's Royal Society of Arts.

Marie Curie

(1867-1934)

Nationality: Polish
Known for: Discoveries and work with radioactivity and radium
Physicist who was also the first woman to win the Nobel Prize.
She won two of the awards – one in Physics and one in Chemistry.
She was one of the pioneers in the discovery and use of x-rays.

Ernest Rutherford

(1871-1937)

Nationality: New Zealand
Known for: The Father of Nuclear Physics. Physicist and chemist
who won the Nobel Prize in 1908 for his work with exploring
radioactive substances. He also had a chemical element named
after him – rutherfordium – which is synthetic and radioactive.

Albert Einstein

(1879-1955)

$$E=mc2$$

Nationality: German
Known for: Theory of Relativity. Einstein was one of the most prominent scientists and physicists in history. He won a Nobel Prize in Physics in 1921 for his law concerning the photoelectric effect. He's also credited with creating the "world's most famous equation."

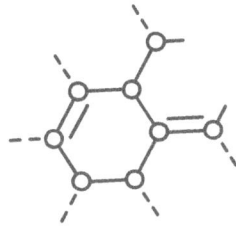

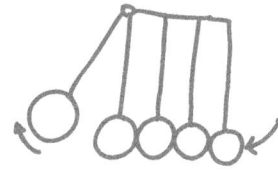

Scientists of the 20th Century

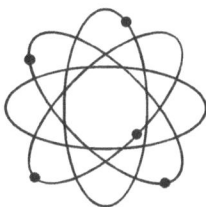

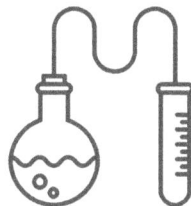

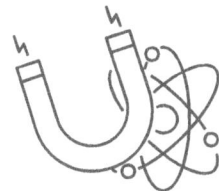

Otto Hahn

(1879-1968)

Nationality: German
Known for: Helped discover nuclear fission Known as the
"Father of Nuclear Chemistry," Hahn studied extensively
the topics of radioactivity and radiochemistry. He was also
a peace activist during WWII.

Alexander Fleming

(1881-1955)

Nationality: Scottish
Known for: Helped create penicillin BIBiologist and pharmacologist who helped discover penicillin which was a medical breakthrough. He shared the Nobel Prize in Physiology for his work with two other people in 1928. This discovery is credited with being the starting point of modern antibiotics.

Niels Bohr

(1885-1962)

Nationality: Danish
Known for: Bohr Model of the Atom Bohr won the Nobel Prize in 1922 in Physics for his work on the atomic structure. He worked towards using atoms for peaceful purposes rather than wartime weapons.He is also credited with creating the principle of complementarity.

Erwin Schrodinger

(1887-1961)

Nationality: Austrian
Known for: One of the founders of quantum physics Shared the Nobel Prize in 1933 for his work in quantum theory. Also did significant work in color theory, cosmology, and other related fields. Published What is Life?, discussing genetics and physics.

Edwin Hubble

(1889-1953)

Nationality: American
Known for: Exploring the Milky Way; Hubble's Law Astronomer
and cosmologist who helped create the field of extragalactic
astronomy. He theorized that the universe is ever-expanding
due to recessional velocity, which was later termed
"Hubble's Law."

Frederick Banting

(1891-1941)

Nationality: Canadian
Known for: Discovered insulin Physician and scientist who won the Nobel Prize in Physics/Medicine in 1923 for discovering insulin. He was the youngest recipient of the prize and he was knighted by King George V in 1934 for his discovery.

Alfred Kinsey

(1894-1956)

Nationality: American
Known for: Studies of Human Sexuality Conducted numerous studies about human sexual nature and opened up the Institute of Sex Research at Indiana Universty. He published Sexual Behavior in the Human Male and Sexual Behavior in the Human Female.

Robert Oppenheimer
(1904-1967)

Nationality: American
Known for: Father of the Atomic Bomb Theoretical physicist who explored nuclear fusion, electrons, positrons and black holes. One of the founders of the American school of theoretical physics and a recipient of the Enrico Fermi Award, given by the US Department of Energy.

Edward Telle

(1908-2003)

Nationality: Hungarian
Known for: Father of the Hydrogen Bomb Theoretical physicist
who supported and advocated for nuclear energy testing and
proliferation. He co-founded the Lawrence Livermore National
Laboratory. Some of his awards include the Albert Einstein
Award and the Enrico Fermi Award.

Alan Turing

(1912-1954)

1
111 0
O 101
100   1
0111101
1111010
1101
1010
0000
1101

1 0
11 101
O   1
1000000
0111101
1111010
1101
1010

Nationality: British
Known for: Pioneer in artificial intelligence and computer science Turin was a mathematician, computer scientist and a codebreaker. He worked for Britain during WWII to create ciphers that helped decode German messages. He has been called the Father of Artificial Intelligence.

Jonas Salk

(1914-1995)

Nationality: American
Known for: Developed the first polio vaccine Medical researcher who spent several years studying the polio virus and finding vaccinations for it. He also studied influenza and searched for ways to cure that. Established the Salk Center for Biological Studies in 1963.

Richard Feynman

(1918-1988)

Nationality: American
Known for: Helped develop the atomic bomb Theoretical physicist who received the Nobel Prize in Physics in 1965 for helping create and develop quantam electrodynamics. He also designed a set of mathematical illustrations concerning subatomic particles, which came to be known as the Feynman Diagrams.

James Watson

(1928)

Nationality: American
Known for: Co-founder of the DNA structure Geneticist and
molecular biologist who was awarded the Nobel Prize in
Physiology in 1962 for his work and collaboration with others
on the molecular structure of DNA.

Carl Sagan

(1934-1996)

Nationality: American
Known for: TV Series Cosmos; exploring extraterrestrial intelligence Astronomer and astrophysicist who wrote several books, co-wrote a TV show about space, and promoted exploration of extraterrestrial intelligence and life. Sagan also had an interest in studying UFOs.

Stephen Hawking

(1942)

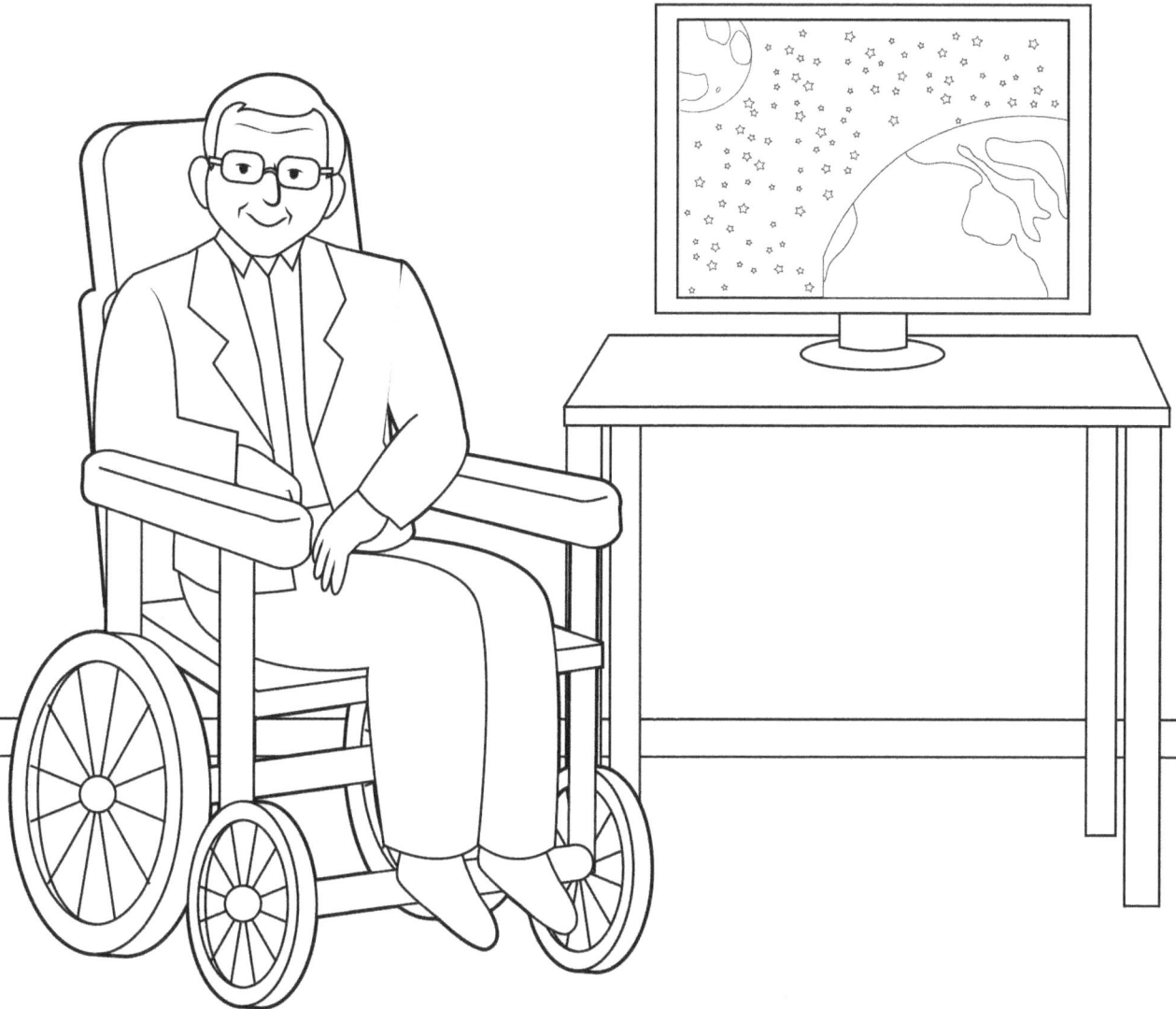

Nationality: British
Known for: Hawking Radiation; Authored A Brief History of Time Cosmologist and theoretical physicist who has studied the phenomenon of black holes and gravity. Honorary Fellow of the Royal Society of Arts. His book, A Brief History of Time, was a bestseller for more than four consecutive years.

www.ingramcontent.com/pod-product-compliance
Lightning Source LLC
Chambersburg PA
CBHW042339030426
42335CB00030B/3401